MAPS AND GLOBES

Fun, Facts, and Activities

BY CAROLINE ARNOLD

Illustrated by Lynn Sweat

An Easy-Read Geography Activity Book

Illustrated with drawings,
photographs,
and diagrams

A GROLIER COMPANY

Franklin Watts

New York   London   Toronto   Sydney

1984

Photographs courtesy of Ginger Giles: p. 10 (top left, top right); © Rand McNally & Co., R.L. 84-S-41: pp. 10 (bottom left, bottom right), 23; Brian Butler: p. 24 (left and right).

R.L. 2.4 Spache Revised Formula

Library of Congress Cataloging in Publication Data

Arnold, Caroline.
Maps and globes.

(An Easy-read geography activity book)
Includes index.
Summary: Explains the uses of maps and globes, with
instructions for making a balloon globe, a model room,
a giant compass rose, a contour map, a treasure map, and
other projects.
1. Maps—Juvenile literature.   2. Globes—Juvenile
literature.   [1. Maps.   2. Globes.   3. Scientific
recreations]   I. Title.   II. Series.
GA105.6.A76 1984   912   84-7595
ISBN 0-531-04720-2

Text copyright © 1984 by Caroline Arnold
Illustrations copyright © 1984 by Franklin Watts, Inc.
Printed in the United States of America
6 5 4 3 2

Contents

Using Maps

What can we find out from maps?
Maps can help us learn where people live,
what people do,
the shape of the land,
how to travel, and
what time it is.

People have been making and using maps for a
    long time.
Explorers, traders, rulers, and soldiers all needed
    maps.
At first their maps were not very good.
But as they found out more about the world, their
    maps became better.
Today people use all kinds of maps every day.
You can learn a lot from maps and have fun, too.

Finding Latitude and Longitude

If you looked at the earth from the moon,
    it would look like a ball floating in space.
A globe is a map of the world drawn on a ball.
A globe shows water and land on the earth.
Water is found in oceans, lakes, and rivers.
The big pieces of land are called continents.
Map makers often draw lines on maps.
These lines help us to find directions, the time,
    and the seasons.
Look at a globe or map of the world.
The North Pole is at the top. The South Pole is at
    the bottom.
You will see many lines that go up and down.
On a globe they meet at the North and South
    poles.
These are called lines of **longitude**.
Around the middle of the globe is a line like a
    belt.
It is the **equator**.
All lines that go around the globe or across the
    map are called lines of **latitude**.
Latitudes north of the equator have winter in January
    and summer in July.
Latitudes south of the equator have winter in July
    and summer in January.
Look at a map or globe.
Find the longitude and latitude of your community.

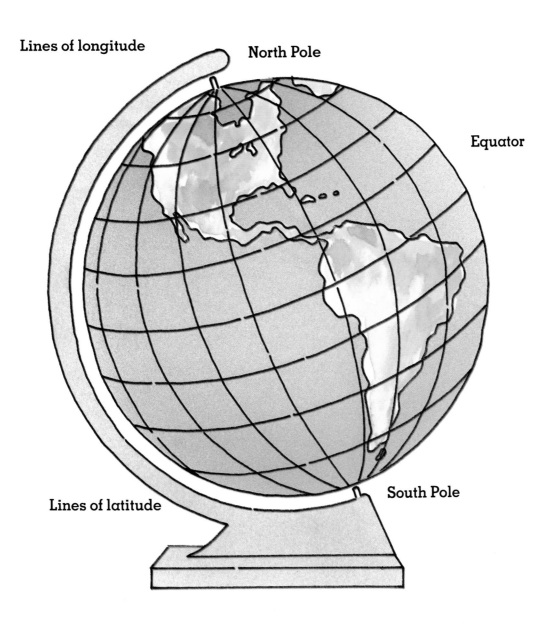

Lines of longitude

North Pole

Equator

Lines of latitude

South Pole

A Balloon Globe

Here is how you can make your own globe.

You will need:
a round balloon (blue is best)
a permanent marker
heavy paper about 6″ (15 cm)
    square
scissors

Blow up the balloon. Tie a knot in it.
The knot is the South Pole.
Draw a small X at the top. This is the North Pole.
Now draw a line around the center of the balloon.
    This is the equator.

Look at a map or globe.
Draw the shapes of the continents on the balloon.
Which continents are above the equator?
Which are below?
Which continents does the equator go through?
Now fold the paper in half.
Make a small cut across the middle of the fold.

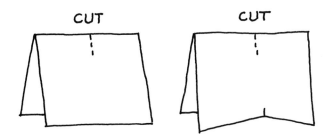

Unfold the paper. Fold it in half the other way.
Make another small cut across the first one.
Open the paper. You will have a small cut X.
Slip the knot of the balloon through the X.
Now your balloon globe will stand by itself.

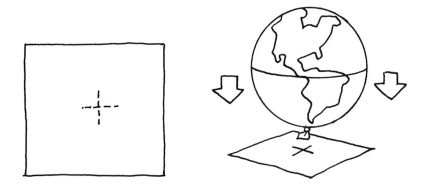

A Model Room

Have you ever seen a model boat or a model plane?
It is a lot like a real boat or plane but smaller.
A map is a model of a place.
The place may be the whole world, a community,
    or even a room.
The **scale** of a map tells you how much smaller
    the map is than what it shows.
One inch (2.5 cm) may be many miles or a few.
On a 16-inch (41-cm) globe 1 inch equals 500
    miles (805 km).
Each of these maps show the city of Chicago.

You can make a model of your room.

On your model 1 inch (2.5 cm) will stand for each
foot (.3 m).

If your room is 12 feet (3.6 m) wide, try to find a
box 12 inches (30 cm) wide.

You will need:
a cardboard box
markers or crayons
building blocks or small boxes

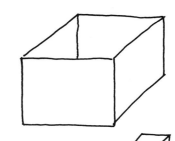

First remove the top of the
box.

Then look around your room.

Where are the doors and windows?

Draw them on the inside of the box.

Draw whatever else you see on the walls of your
room.

Use the blocks or boxes for furniture.

Imagine how small you would have to be to live
in your model room!

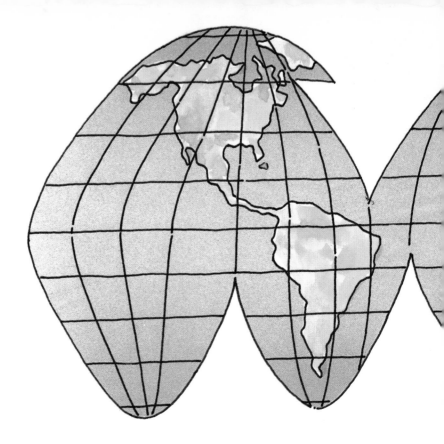

Making the Round Earth Flat
Orange-Peel Experiment

A long time ago people thought the earth was flat.
Today we know that the earth is round.
How do map makers draw a round shape on flat
　　paper?
Sometimes they make the map look as if the earth
　　has been cut into sections.
You can see how they do it with an orange.

You will need:
one orange (try to use one that peels easily)
a table knife

Use the knife to cut just
    the skin of the orange.
Make two circles to divide the
    orange into fourths.
Now carefully peel the skin off the orange.
Put the pieces side by side.
Do they look something like this map?
Maps like this are close to being true. But some-
    times they can be hard to read.

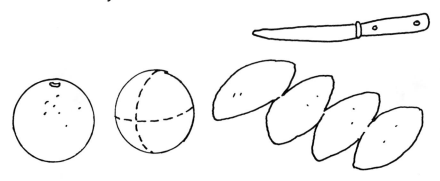

Stretching the Globe

Sometimes map makers "stretch" parts of the
    model earth to make it flat.
You can see how they do this with a balloon
    globe.

You will need:
a balloon globe
scissors

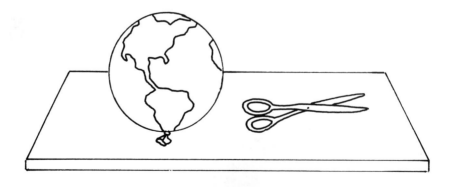

Let the air out of the balloon.
Carefully cut the balloon in half.
Now stretch each side.
Try to make the balloon lie flat.
You can see that the shapes of the continents
    change a lot at the edges of the balloon.

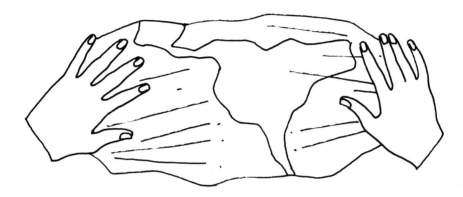

"Stretched" maps of the world are most true in the
    center.
Now cut out "Australia."
Try to make it flat.
It is easier to make flat maps of smaller areas.

Map Keys Unlock Map Secrets

All maps are written in a kind of code.
The map key helps you to read this code.
Signs or pictures show such things as roads, train
      tracks, airports, schools, or parks.
Here is a map of a community.
How many schools do you see?
Can you use some of the same signs and pictures
      to make your own map?
Your map can be of a real or imaginary place.
Be sure to include a map key.

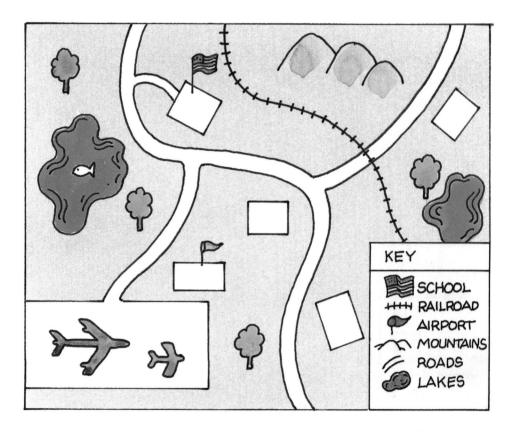

Make a Giant Compass Rose

People who make maps need to find directions.
You can use a compass to find directions.
Inside a compass is a small iron needle.
The North Pole is a giant magnet in the earth.
It pulls at the needle in the compass.
It makes the needle point north.
On most maps north is at the top.
South is at the bottom.
East is on the right.
And west is on the left.
Look at a map of the United States.
What states are on the east coast?
What states are on the west coast?
On most maps there is a sign pointing to north.
It may be an arrow.

Or it may be a **compass rose**.
A compass rose shows all the directions.
You can use a compass to make a giant compass
  rose.

You will need:
a compass
chalk
a large paved area like a play-
  ground

Some playgrounds have circles on them for
  games.
If not, draw a giant circle with chalk.
Put down the compass in the center of the circle.
Make sure it is level.
Wait until the needle is still.
Now turn the compass until the needle and the
  compass point north.
At north draw a line to the edge of the circle.
Write the word "north" there.
Draw lines to the other directions too.
Write "south," "east," and "west."
Now stand on the edge of the circle.
Face out toward your house.
Look on your giant compass rose.
What direction are you facing?

Sun Directions

You can use the sun to find directions too.

You will need:
four pieces of paper
a crayon or marker
tape

The sun rises in the east.
It sets in the west.
Where does the sun shine into your house in the
    morning?

That side of your house faces east.
Write the letter E on a piece of paper.
Put it on the east wall.
The wall across from that is the west wall.
Put a paper with a W on it there.
Stand and face the east wall.
The wall on your right is south.
On your left is north.
Put an N on the north wall and an S on the south
    wall.
Now you can find your directions at any time of
    day.

Star Directions

How can you find directions if the sun is not shin-
ing?

At night you can look at the sky.

People north of the equator look for the North Star.

People south of the equator look for the Southern
Cross.

These stars are always in the north or south.

Go outside on a clear night.

Have an adult help you try to find these stars.

Remember that the cup of the Big Dipper always
points to the North Star.

The North Star is at the end of the handle of the
Little Dipper.

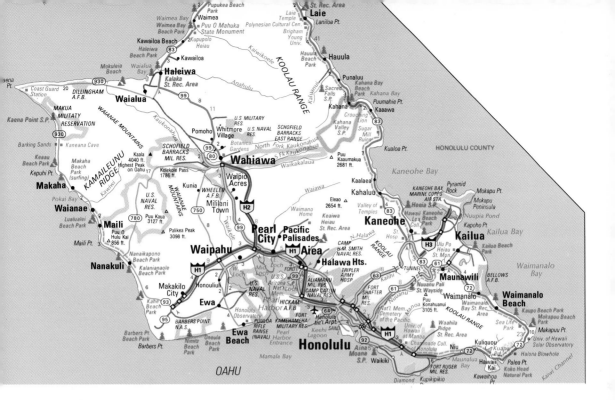

Road Maps

Road maps help us to get from one place to another by car.

On maps of large areas cities and towns are usually shown by dots.

Roads are usually shown by lines.

Different kinds of roads are often different widths or different colors.

Here is a map of the island of Oahu in Hawaii.

Can you find three different ways to travel from Honolulu to Kailua?

Signs along the road help us to find our place on a map.

The next time you go on a trip you can look at signs and maps.

You can help to choose which way to go.

Making Hills and Valleys

Maps that show the shape of the land are called
    contour maps.

Some contour maps are made with lines.

Lines that are close together show hills that are
    very steep.

Lines that are far apart show gentle slopes.

On some maps changes in height are shown with
    colors.

The colors are not always the same on all maps.

Usually blue is for water.

Green is for lowlands (up to 300 meters [984 feet]).

Yellow is for low hills (between 300 meters [984
    feet] and 500 meters [1,640 feet]).

Brown is for high hills (between 500 meters [1,640
    feet] and 2,000 meters [6,562 feet]).

Red is for mountains (above 2,000 meters [6,562
    feet]).

You can make your own contour map.

You will need:	two paper clips
tracing paper	a pencil
scissors	crayons or colored pencils

Cut the tracing paper to the size of this page.

Use the paper clips to fasten the tracing paper to the page.

Trace the map with the pencil.

Then use the crayons or colored pencils to color the mountains and valleys.

You can tell what color to use by looking at the numbers inside each area.

What Time Is It Where You Live?

The earth is like a giant ball spinning in the sky.
It is day on the side facing the sun.
It is night on the side facing away from the sun.
The earth has 24 time zones.
In each zone it is a different time of day or night.
Here is a map of the time
zones in the United
States.
What time zone do you
live in?

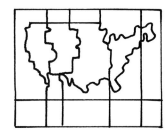

You can find out the time in other time zones with
a paper-plate clock.

You will need: paper
a paper plate   scissors
a pencil   a brad or small nail

Write the number 12 at the top of the plate.
Write the number 6 on the bottom of the plate.
Write the other numbers in between.
The plate will look like a clock face.
Now cut two strips of paper 4 (10 cm) and 3
inches (7.5 cm) long.
Cut one end on each strip to make a point.
Use the brad to fasten the strips of paper to the
center of the plate.

These are the hands of your clock.

Now move the hands to say what time it is where you live.

You can find out the time in the time zone to your east by moving the hour hand one hour ahead.

Move it one hour behind to find out the time one zone to your west.

What time is it in New York when it is one o'clock in California?

New York and California are three time zones apart.

You must move your hour hand ahead three hours to find out.

Make a Treasure Map

Communities are always changing.
People move, roads and bridges are made, and
buildings are built and torn down.
When communities change, maps change too.
Here is a map of the United States 250 years ago.
How is it different from maps today?
Look at some old maps.
How has your community changed?

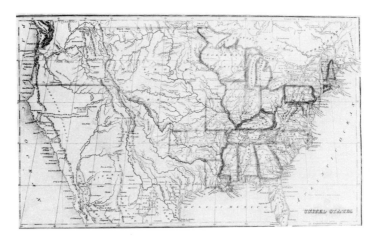

You can make a pretend treasure map that looks
old.

You will need:
a piece of white paper
1/2 cup of cold coffee
a brown or black marker pen

First tear a small strip off each edge of the paper
to give your map a ragged edge.

Then crumple the paper into a ball.
Now smooth it out to make it flat again.
Dip the edges of the paper in the coffee.
They will turn brown.
Let them dry.
Now draw a pretend map in the
    middle of the paper.
Where did you hide your pretend
    buried treasure?

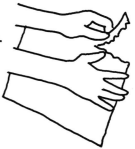

Maps have been around a long time.
The oldest known map was made over 4,000 years
    ago in ancient Babylon.
Some of the first maps were made by explorers.
They needed maps so they would not get lost.
Traders needed maps to know where to sell their
    goods.
Kings and armies needed maps to plan battles.
Today people use all kinds of maps every day.
Maps help us to learn about the world we live in.

Words to Know

Compass Rose. A representation of a compass that shows all the directions.

Continent. A large piece of land on the globe. The world is usually divided into seven continents: Africa, Antarctica, Asia, Australia, Europe, North America, and South America.

Contour Map. A special map that shows the shape and surfaces of land.

Equator. A line, like a belt, around the middle of a map or globe.

Globe. A map of the world drawn on a ball. A globe shows land and water.

Key. Pictures or symbols on a map that help you to understand the map.

Latitude. Lines that go across a map or around a globe are called lines of latitude.

Longitude. Lines on a map or globe that go up or down are called lines of longitude.

Map. A drawing, or model, of a place.

North Pole. The area at the top of a globe or map. Lines of longitude meet at the North Pole.

Road Maps. Special maps that show how to get from one place to another.

Scale. A way to measure on a map. Scale tells you how much smaller the map is than what it shows.

South Pole. The area at the bottom of a globe or map. Lines of longitude meet at the South Pole.

Time Zone. A division of different times of day or night. There are twenty-four time zones throughout the world.

Index